Aural Time!

Practice Tests for the New Revised ABRSM Syllabus and Other Exams

Grade 4

DAVID TURNBULL

CONTENTS

Published by
Bosworth & Co. Limited
14-15 Berners Street,
London W1T 3LJ, UK.

Exclusive Distributors:
Music Sales Limited
Distribution Centre, Newmarket Road,
Bury St Edmunds, Suffolk IP33 3YB, UK.
Music Sales Pty Limited
20 Resolution Drive, Caringbah,
NSW 2229, Australia.

Order No. BOE100089
ISBN 978-1-84938-760-6

Printed in the EU.

Your Guarantee of Quality
As publishers, we strive to produce every book to the
highest commercial standards.
This book has been carefully designed to minimise awkward
page turns and to make playing from it a real pleasure.
Particular care has been given to specifying acid-free, neutral-sized
paper made from pulps which have not been elemental chlorine bleached.
This pulp is from farmed sustainable forests and was
produced with special regard for the environment.
Throughout, the printing and binding have been planned to ensure
a sturdy, attractive publication which should give years of enjoyment.
If your copy fails to meet our high standards,
please inform us and we will gladly replace it.

www.musicsales.com

BOSWORTH
part of The Music Sales Group

INTRODUCTION

Attentive listening is one of the most important skills in music-making, but many teachers will know pupils who convince themselves that they cannot do aural. This can easily happen if listening skills are left until the busy final weeks before an examination. Pupils easily lose confidence when faced with complete practice tests for which they have had little preparation. Many teachers start work for a new grade by beginning with the pieces, but there is no obligation to do so. Sometimes it can be more profitable to start with the aural requirements and other supporting tests (sight-reading, scales and arpeggios), aiming for real security in these areas as an incentive to begin tackling the prepared pieces.

To supplement aural work in lesson time, pupils can be encouraged to explore web sites and commercial CDs that offer suitable exercises, and to team-up with friends to test each other. They might also enjoy keeping a 'listening diary' of pieces that they've heard on the radio or on the Internet, noting points about features of the music that are relevant to the test in Section C (tonality, tempo, character and so on).

Once it is time for more formal aural training, the late David Turnbull's popular *Aural Time!* series provides ample and highly regarded practice materials. This new edition coincides with the introduction of some small changes to the aural requirements of the Associated Board of the Royal Schools of Music examinations, effective from January 2011 onwards.

At Grade 4, the only significant change is to questions in Test C(i) on the character of the music. Examiners will ask something like, 'What in the music gives this piece its character?' to make it clear that candidates must mention musical features in their response. In the early stages of preparation many pupils, especially younger ones, will need help in articulating concepts about which they may not have previously given much thought. Could it be jolly dotted rhythms and staccato articulation, calm dynamics and a song-like melody, thick chords in a sombre minor key, the decisive beat and firm dynamics of a march, or the regular phrases and clear rhythms of a dance? It may help pupils to begin preparation for this test by discussing pieces that they have learnt in the past, asking them to describe the character of the music and to identify which musical features help create that mood or character.

Pupils who have worked through the earlier grades should be gaining confidence by now in tests that require a sung response. However, for those who find this a worry, it is worth emphasising that the examiner is only interested in accurate pitch – vocal tone does not matter. Boys with changing voices may sing an octave lower and candidates may whistle or hum if that is easier. Remember that answers to Test A can be played rather than sung, in which case, the examiner will name the key chord and starting note.

In Test B, pupils should be encouraged not to rush through the five notes required – each should be sustained for a second or two (something that nervous singers often find difficult). Teachers should interrupt the singing if any note is incorrectly pitched by saying, for example, "no, the third note should be …" and then playing the correct pitch. Pupils need to be aware that a similar interruption is likely to occur in the examination, as this type of test can rarely be completed accurately once an interval has been wrongly pitched. Those that find this type of test difficult will benefit by starting with the 36 very simple, graded examples at the start of Section B of this volume.

Paul Terry
London, 2010

A Note about Musical Features

In many types of music examination pupils are asked about features of a piece of music played. These include **rhythm, melody, dynamics** (including gradations of dynamics like *crescendo* and *diminuendo*, **articulation** of notes, **tempo** (including changes to tempo), **tonality** (the choice of **keys**), **harmony**, the **texture** of the music, particularly homophony and counterpoint, and the general **form** of the piece being examined. Questions of this type appear in the ABRSM Grade 4 examination as well as in others, and teachers sometimes ask for further guidance.

The way the composer uses these features gives to a piece its **character**. For example, if a piece is slow in tempo, is written in a minor key, has articulation which is largely *legato* and has dynamics which are mostly *piano*, the character of the music is likely to be sad. If a piece of music is fast in tempo, in a major key, has articulation which is sometimes *staccato* and dynamics which are often *forte*, the character of the music is likely to seem bright and cheerful.

Test A. Memorising Melodies

GRADE 4

These melodies will be played twice. The keychord and the starting note will be played and named. The pulse will be tapped. Pupils may then **either** sing **or** play the melodies.

Sometimes, pupils find at first that they cannot remember all of a melody. Teachers may like to divide some melodies into phrases to help.

2

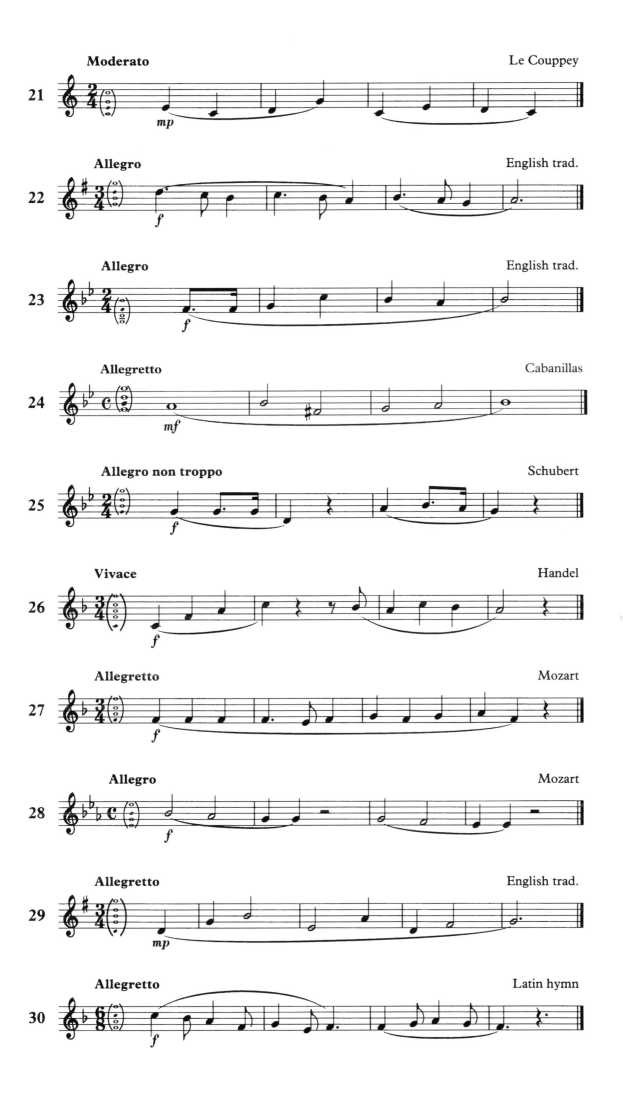

4

Test B. Sight-Singing in Free Time

These excercises are to be sung at sight in free time. The keychord and the keynote will be given. Any wrong notes will be corrected at the keyboard.

In examinations they are sung to vowels or 'lah', but they also make excellent practice for general aural development for GCSE and other work if they are sung to their letter names or sol-fa names.

Tests are written in treble and bass clefs, and pupils may choose which clef they wish to use in an examination. When practising, however, pupils can also be encouraged to sing from *both* clefs, transposing the starting note down or up an octave as necessary, so that note reading becomes equally fluent in treble and the bass clefs. As well as practising these tests with their teacher, pupils can also be encouraged to practise them on their own, giving themselves keychords and checking their notes with their instrument.

Pupils may have had little previous experience of sight singing, so Exercises 1-36 are very simple. Exercises 37-70 are similar to those which may be found in examinations.

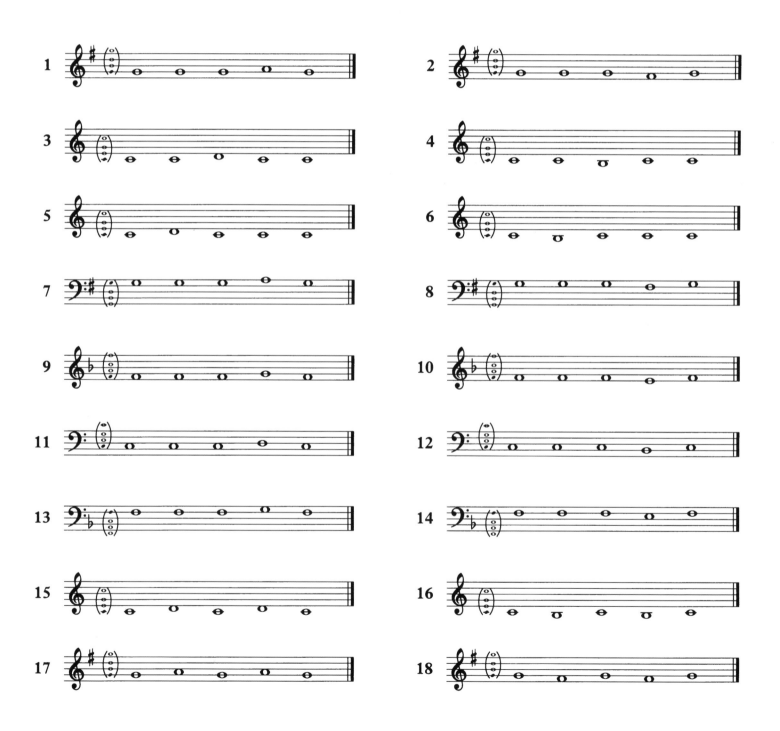

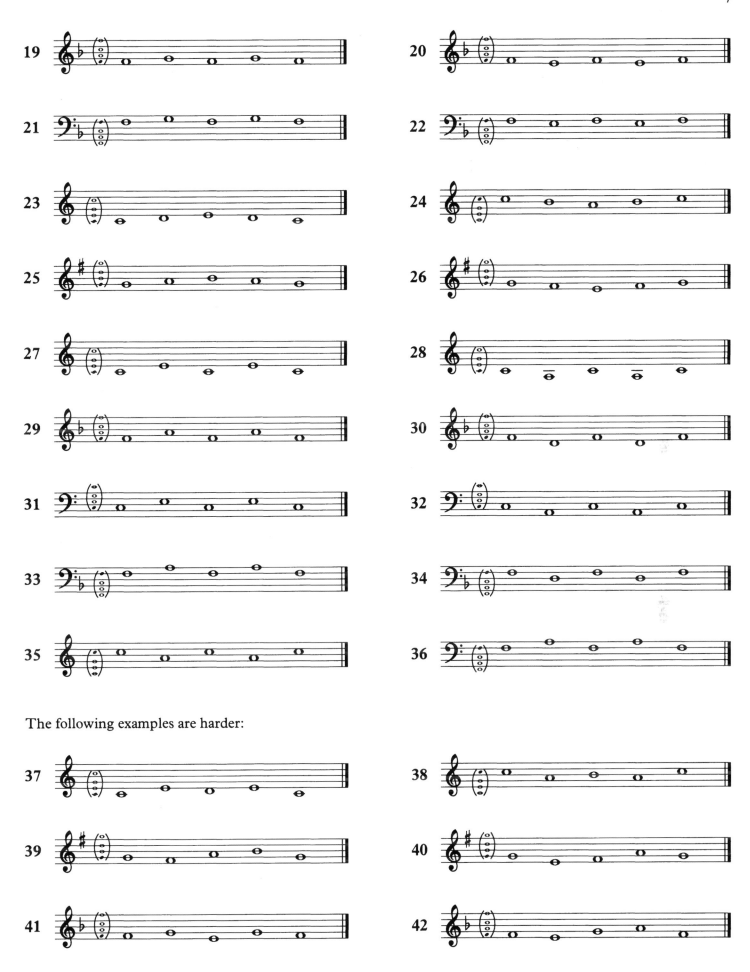

The following examples are harder:

8

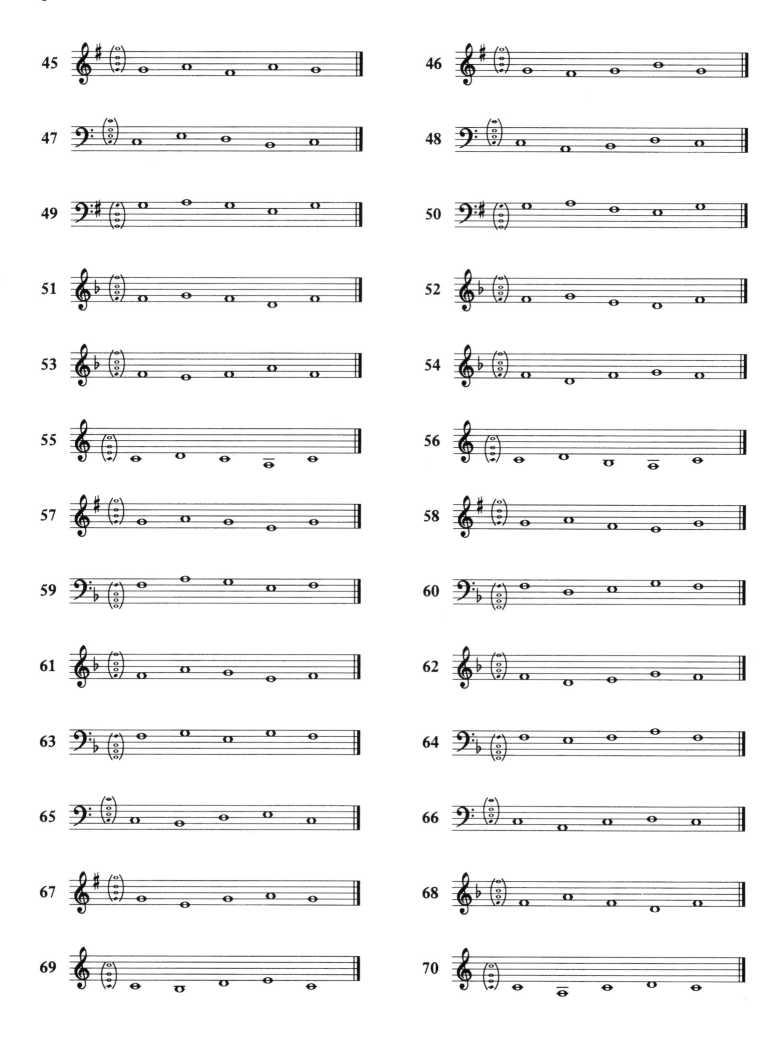

Test C1. Recognising Features.

To the pupil.

You will be asked to comment on two of the following features of pieces in this section:

dynamics (*p/f*), and **gradation of dynamics** (*crescendo/diminuendo*),

articulation of notes (*legato/staccato*);

tempo including changes to tempo (*rallentando, accelerando* etc.);

the recognition of whether the **tonality** (key) is major or minor;

the **character** of the music played.

You will be told which two features you will be questioned on before the piece is played.

Test C2. Clapping rhythms

Your teacher will play twice a short extract from the piece used in C1. You must clap back its rhythm, and say if it is in two, three of four time.

To the teacher. For the C2 clapping, two phrases are printed from which you can choose **one**.

C1 *Questions*

a. Is the **tonality** major or minor?

b. Describe the **character** of the piece.

c. Does the **tempo** alter, or stay the same?

d. Do the **dynamics** alter during the piece? If so, where?

C2 Clap this extract, which will be played twice. After you have clapped it, say if it is in two time, three time or four time.

Tempo di Marcia

Mozart: From *"Marriage of Figaro"*

C1 *Questions*

    a. Is the **tonality** major or minor?

    b. Describe the **character** of the piece. Is it like a march, or a dance? Bright, or sad?

    c. Does the **tempo** alter, or stay the same?

    d. Do the **dynamics** alter during the piece? If so, where?

C2 Clap this extract, which will be played twice. After you have clapped it, say if it is in two time, three time or four time.

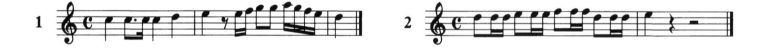

C1 *Questions*

    a. Is the **tonality** major or minor?

    b. Describe the **character** of the piece.

    c. Does the **tempo** alter, or stay the same?

    d. Do the **dynamics** alter during the piece? If so, where?

    e. Comment on the **articulation** (*legato/staccato*).

C2 Clap this extract, which will be played twice. After you have clapped it, say if it is in two time, three time or four time.

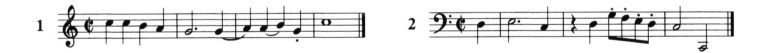

Delibes arr. Heumann

C1 *Questions*

    a. Is the **tonality** major or minor?

    b. Describe the **character** of the piece.

    c. Does the **tempo** alter, or stay the same?

    d. Do the **dynamics** alter during the piece? If so, where?

    e. Is the **articulation** *staccato* or *legato*?

C2 Clap this extract, which will be played twice. After you have clapped it, say if it is in two time, three time or four time.

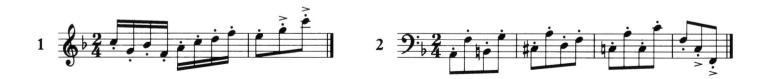

C1 *Questions*

a. Is the **tonality** major or minor?
b. Describe the **character** of the piece.
c. Does the **tempo** alter, or stay the same?
d. Describe the **dynamics** of the piece.
e. Is the **articulation** at the end *legato* or *staccato*. How does it start?

C2 Clap this extract, which will be played twice. After you have clapped it, say if it is in two time, three time or four time.

C1 *Questions*
a. Is the **tonality** mostly major or minor?
b. Describe the **character** of the piece.
c. Does the **tempo** alter, or stay the same?
d. Describe the **dynamics**. Does it start softly or loudly? How does it continue?

C2 Clap this extract, which will be played twice. After you have clapped it, say if it is in two time, three time or four time.

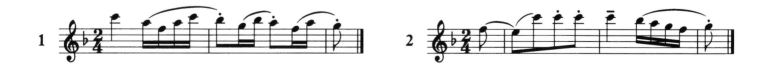

Molto sostenuto   Handel

C1 *Questions*

    a. Is the **tonality** mostly major or minor?

    b. Describe the **character** and mood of the piece.

    c. Does the **tempo** alter, or stay the same? If it changes, where does this happen?

    d. Describe the **dynamics**.

    e. Is the **articulation** *legato* or *staccato*.

C2 Clap this extract, which will be played twice. After you have clapped it, say if it is in two time, three time or four time.

Andante   Kirchner

C1 *Questions*

    a. Is the **tonality** of this major or minor?

    b. Describe the **character** and mood of the piece.

    c. Does the **tempo** alter. If so, how and where?

    d. Describe the **dynamics**.

    e. Is the **articulation** *legato* or *staccato*.

C2 Clap this extract, which will be played twice. After you have clapped it, say if it is in two time, three time or four time.

Beethoven

C1 Questions

    a. Is the **tonality** at the beginning of this major or minor? Does it change? If so, where?

    b. Does the **character** of the piece stay the same, or does the mood change?

    c. Does the **tempo** alter. If so, how and where?

    d. Describe the **dynamics**.

    e. Is the **articulation** *legato* or *staccato*. Does it alter?

C2 Clap this extract, which will be played twice. After you have clapped it, say if it is in two time, three time or four time.

Allegro

Wagner: Ride of the Valkyries

C1 *Questions*

    a. Is the **tonality** at the start major, or minor?
       Are there any alterations in the middle of the piece?
    b. How would you describe the **character** and mood of the music.
    c. Does the **tempo** alter. If so, how and where?
    d. Do the **dynamics** change? If so, where?

C2 Clap this extract, which will be played twice. After you have clapped it, say if it is in two time, three time or four time.

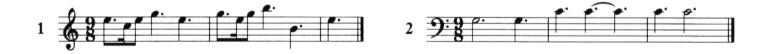

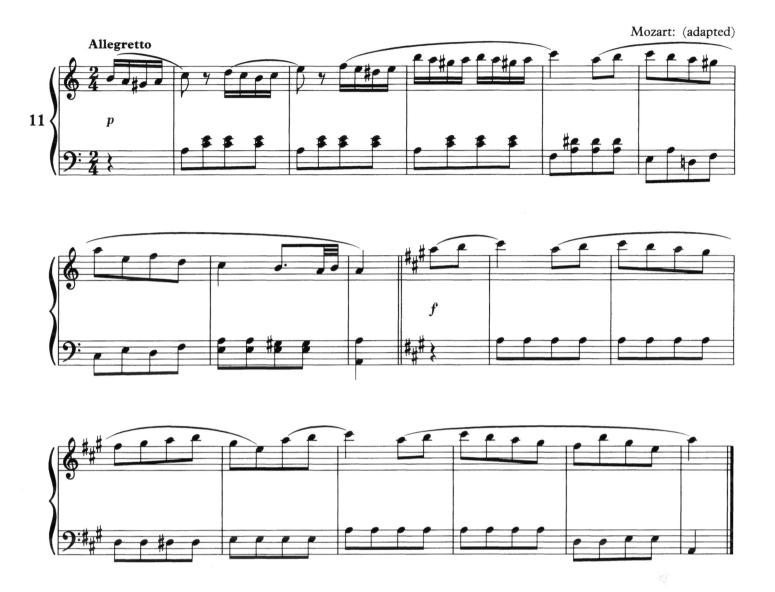

Mozart: (adapted)

C1 *Questions*

    a. Is the **tonality** at the start major, or minor?

    b. Does it end in a major or minor **key**?

    c. Describe the **character** of the piece.

    d. Describe the **dynamics** used.

    e. Does the **tempo** of the piece change? If so, how?

C2 Clap this extract, which will be played twice. After you have clapped it, say if it is in two time, three time or four time.

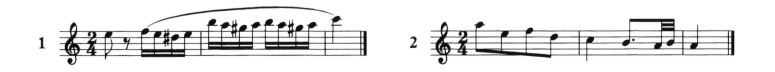

C1 *Questions*

a. Is the **tonality** major or minor?
b. How would you describe the **character** and mood of the music?
c. Does the **tempo** alter. If so, how and where?
d. Do the **dynamics** change? If so, where?

C2 Clap this extract, which will be played twice. After you have clapped it, say if it is in two time, three time or four time.

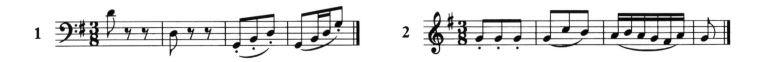

C1 *Questions*
   a. Are the **dynamics** at the end loud or soft?
   b. Is the **tonality** mainly major, or minor?
   c. Does the **key** change ever? If so, where?
   d. Is the **tempo** held steady, or does it change?
   e. Describe the **character** and mood of the music.

C2 Clap this extract, which will be played twice. After you have clapped it, say if it is in two time, three time or four time.

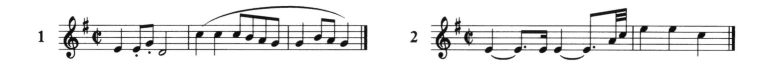

Andante ♩ = 84

Beethoven

C1 *Questions*

 a. Is the **tonality** mostly major or minor?
 b. Is the **articulation** at the beginning *legato* or *staccato*?
 c. Are there any changes in **tempo**? If so, where?
 d. Discuss the **dynamics** of the last four-bar phrase?

C2 Clap this extract, which will be played twice. After you have clapped it, say if it is in two time, three time or four time.

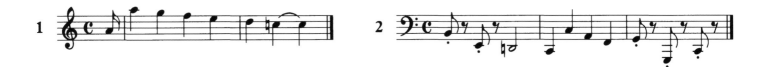

Allegro

Dandrieu (adapted)

15

p

f

senza rit.

C1 *Questions*

    a. Is the **articulation** at the start *legato* or *staccato*?
    b. Is the **tonality** major, or minor?
    c. Describe the **character** and mood of the music.
    d. Is there any change in **tempo**?
    e. Describe any changes in **dynamics**.

C2 Clap this extract, which will be played twice. After you have clapped it, say if it is in two time, three time or four time.

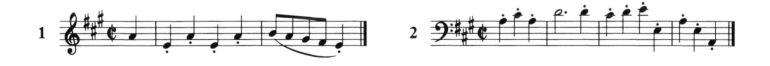

1

2

Allegro   Attwood (adapted)

16

C1 *Questions*

a. Describe the **dynamics** of the music.
b. Are there any changes in **tempo**? If so, where do they occur?
c. Is the **tonality** major, or minor?
d. Is the **articulation** of the first notes of the melody *legato* or *staccato*?
e. Describe the **character** and mood of the music.

C2 Clap this extract, which will be played twice. After you have clapped it, say if it is in two time, three time or four time.

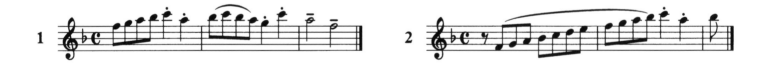

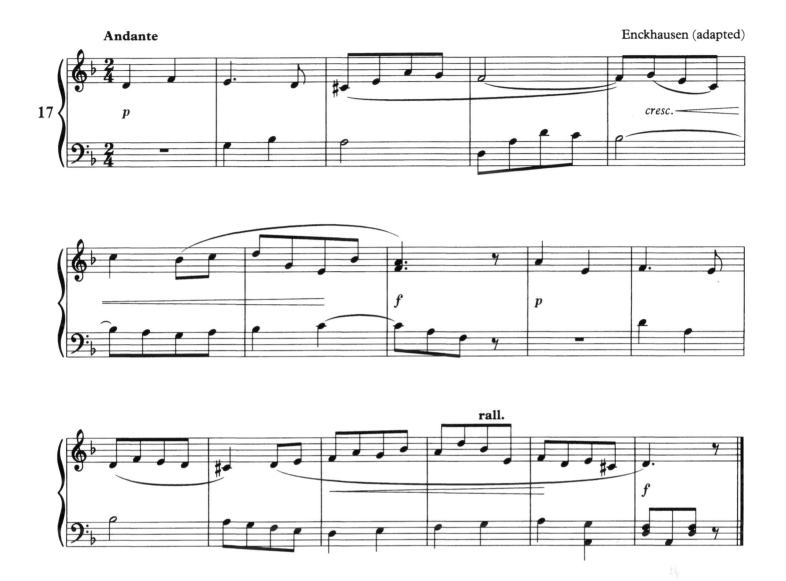

C1 *Questions*
    a. Does the music start in a major or a minor **key**?
    b. Does the **tonality** change at all? If so, where?
    c. Are there any modifications to the **tempo**? If so, where?
    d. Describe any changes in **dynamics**.
    e. Is the **articulation** of this piece mostly *legato* or *staccato*?

C2 Clap this extract, which will be played twice. After you have clapped it, say if it is in two time, three time or four time.

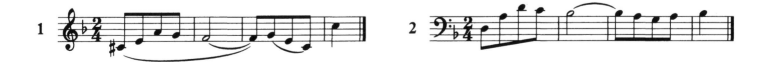

Allegro tranquillo

Schütt (adapted)

C1 *Questions*
a. Describe any changes of **tempo**.
b. Comment on the **character** and mood of the music.
c. Describe the **dynamics** used in the music.
d. Is the **tonality** at the start major, or minor?
e. Is the music mostly *staccato* or *legato* in its **articulation**?

C2 Clap this extract, which will be played twice. After you have clapped it, say if it is in two time, three time or four time.

C1 *Questions*

    a. Is the **tonality** major, or minor?

    b. Describe any changes in **tempo**.

    c. Is the **articulation** of the first note of the melody *staccato* or *legato*?

    d. Describe the **character** and style of the music.

    e. Does the first strong accent fall on the first note? If not, on which note does it fall?

C2 Clap this extract, which will be played twice. After you have clapped it, say if it is in two time, three time or four time.

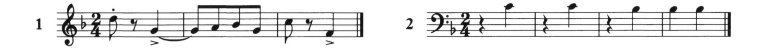

C1 *Questions*

    a. Describe the **character** and mood of this music.

    b. Are there any changes in **tempo**?

    c. Is the **tonality** major, or minor?

    d. Is the **articulation** just before the end *legato* or *staccato*?

C2 Clap this extract, which will be played twice. After you have clapped it, say if it is in two time, three time or four time.

Other titles by David Turnbull...

Available from

BOSWORTH
part of The Music Sales Group

Exclusive Distributors:
Music Sales Limited
Distribution Centre, Newmarket Road,
Bury St Edmunds, Suffolk IP33 3YB, UK.

www.musicsales.com